Entire contents copyright © 2012 Uncensored Classics
All rights reserved

Book design and Introduction by S. C. Torode

Printed in the USA

ON
MASTURBATION

UNCENSORED CLASSICS

INTRODUCTION

On a tour of Europe, Mark Twain noted that "France has neither winter nor summer nor morals." It was in true French spirit, then, that he composed and delivered his 1879 speech to a Parisian men's club, "Some Thoughts on the Science of Onanism."

That evening, Twain grappled with a most pressing concern and demonstrated his complete mastery of the subject at hand.

Before delving into Twain's text, however, some historical perspective is needed to grasp why his words were shocking at the time, and why the speech was censored for many years.

After reaching its height of popularity in ancient Rome, masturbation was condemned by the early Church Fathers. They read in their Bibles of Onan, who spilled his semen on the ground, and was slain by God for this wicked offense. (Hence the term "Onanism.") In order to avoid sharing Onan's fate, Christian monks "mortified the flesh" by bathing in ice-cold water. Some went so far as to castrate themselves. (Ironically, it was masturbation, not self-maiming, that the Church dubbed "self-abuse.") The author of the second-century Letter of Barnabas said of the unruly penis, "Moses rightly detested the weasel." *

In the Middle Ages, the Catholic Church declared masturbation a mortal sin worthy of eternal damnation—a judgement it still holds today.

As much as they hated the Pope, the Protestant Reformers hated Onan even more. "The exceedingly foul deed of Onan," Martin Luther fumed, "is far more atrocious than incest or adultery."

In Mark Twain's day, doctors warned that while God might not personally slay those guilty of Onanism, its ill effects would surely lead to an early death. This admonition from a 1903 medical text is typical:

---

* Unlike the fictitious quotations in Twain's speech, all the quotes in this introduction are genuine.

ON MASTURBATION

Teach your boy that when he handles or excites the sexual organs, all parts of the body suffer. This is why it is called "self-abuse." The sin is terrible, and is, in fact, worse than lying or stealing. For, although these are wicked and will ruin the soul, self-abuse will ruin both soul and body. This loathsome habit lays the foundation for consumption, paralysis, and heart disease. It makes many boys lose their minds; others, when grown, commit suicide.

Victorian newspapers advertised male chastity belts, pills to reduce sexual desire, and even metal clamps to put the squeeze on erections. Under society's stern, disapproving gaze, masculinity withered in impotence.

Amidst all this repression, Mark Twain took a lone stand. He whipped out his satirical pen and rose to the defense of the much-maligned member, suggesting that true manliness entails more than just a stiff upper lip.

Here follows Mark Twain's pubic declaration of independence.

—S. C. TORODE
author of *The Dirty Parts of the Bible*

SOME THOUGHTS ON THE SCIENCE OF ONANISM

My gifted predecessor has warned you against the "social evil—adultery." In his able paper he exhausted that subject; he left absolutely nothing more to be said on it. But I will continue his good work in the of morality by cautioning you against that species of recreation called self-abuse—to which I perceive that you are too much addicted.

MARK TWAIN

All great writers upon health and morals, both ancient and modern, have struggled with this stately subject; this shows its dignity and importance. Some of these writers have taken one side, some the other.

ON MASTURBATION

Homer, in the second book of the Iliad, says with fine enthusiasm, "Give me masturbation or give me death!"

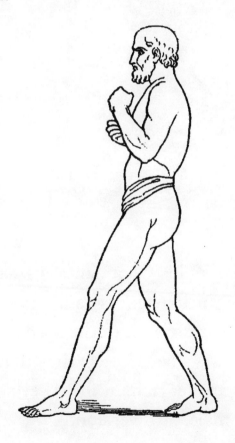

MARK TWAIN

Caesar, in his Commentaries, says, "To the lonely it is company; to the forsaken it is a friend; to the aged and impotent it is a benefactor; they that be penniless are yet rich, in that they still have this majestic diversion."

ON MASTURBATION

In another place this excellent observer has said, "There are times when I prefer it to sodomy."

Robinson Crusoe says, "I cannot describe what I owe to this gentle art."

MARK TWAIN

Queen Elizabeth said, "It is the bulwark of virginity."

ON MASTURBATION

Cetewayo, the Zulu hero, remarked that, "A jerk in the hand is worth two in the bush."

The immortal Franklin has said, "Masturbation is the mother of invention." He also said, "Masturbation is the best policy."

ON MASTURBATION

Michelangelo and all the other Old Masters—Old Masters, I will remark, is an abbreviation, a contraction—have used similar language. Michelangelo said to Pope Julius II, "Self-negation is noble, self-culture is beneficent, self-possession is manly, but to the truly great and inspiring soul they are poor and tame compared to self-abuse."

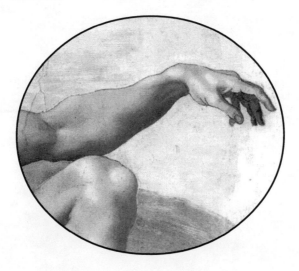

Mr. Browning, in one of his latest and most graceful poems refers to it in an eloquent line which is destined to live to the end of time, "None know it but to love it, None name it but to praise."

ON MASTURBATION

Such are the utterances of the most illustrious of the masters of this renowned science, and apologists for it. The name of those who decry it and oppose it is legion; they have made strong arguments and uttered bitter speeches against it.

MARK TWAIN

Brigham Young, an expert of incontestable authority, said, "As compared with the other thing, it is the difference between the lightning bug and the lightning."

ON MASTURBATION

S olomon said, "There is nothing to recommend it but its cheapness."

Galen said, "It is shameful to degrade to such bestial use that grand limb, that formidable member, which we votaries of science dub the 'Major Maxillary'—when we dub it at all, which is seldom. It would be better to decapitate the Major than to use him so. It would be better to amputate the *os frontis* than to put it to such a use."

ON MASTURBATION

The great statistician, Smith, in his Report to Parliament, says, "In my opinion, more children have been wasted in this way than in any other. It cannot be denied that the high authority of this art entitles it to our respect; but at the same time I think that its harmfulness demands our condemnation."

Mr. Darwin was grieved to feel obliged to give up his theory that the monkey was the connecting link between man and the lower animals. I think he was too hasty.

ON MASTURBATION

The monkey is the only animal, except man, that practices this science; hence he is our brother; there is a bond of sympathy and relationship between us. Give this ingenious animal an audience of the proper kind, and he will straightway put aside his other affairs and take a whet; and you will see by the contortions and his ecstatic expression that he takes an intelligent and human interest in his performance.

The signs of excessive indulgence in this destructive pastime are easily detectable. They are these: A disposition to eat, to drink, to smoke, to meet together convivially, to laugh, to joke, and tell indelicate stories— and mainly, a yearning to paint pictures.

ON MASTURBATION

The results of the habit are: Loss of memory, loss of virility, loss of cheerfulness, loss of hopefulness, loss of character, and loss of progeny.

Of all the various kinds of sexual intercourse, this has the least to recommend it. As an amusement it is too fleeting; as an occupation it is too wearing; as a public exhibition there is no money in it. It is unsuited to the drawing room, and in the most cultured society it has long since been banished from the social board.

ON MASTURBATION

It has at last, in our day of progress and improvement, been degraded to brotherhood with flatulence—among the best bred these two arts are now indulged only in private—though by consent of the whole company, when only males are present, it is still permissible, in good society, to remove the embargo upon the fundamental sigh.

My illustrious predecessor has taught you that all forms of the 'social evil' are bad. I would teach you that some of those forms are more to be avoided than others; so, in concluding, I say: If you must gamble away your life sexually, don't play a Lone Hand too much.

ON MASTURBATION

When you feel a revolutionary uprising in your system, get your Vendome Column down some other way—don't jerk it down.

Mark Twain

Made in the USA
San Bernardino, CA
15 March 2014